W9-ANR-901

COLUMBIA CENTRAL H.S. LIBRARY
BROOKLYN, MICH.

Jonestown Massacre

IN MEMORY OF
THE VICTIMS OF
THE JONESTOWN TRAGEDY
NOV. 18, 1978
JONESTOWN, GUYANA
GUYANA EMERGENCY
RELIEF COMMITTEE

Other titles in the *American Disasters* series:

Apollo 1 Tragedy
Fire in the Capsule
ISBN 0-7660-1787-7

Attack on America
The Day the Twin
Towers Collapsed
ISBN 0-7660-2118-1

The Challenger Disaster
Tragic Space Flight
ISBN 0-7660-1222-0

Columbine High School Shooting
Student Violence
ISBN 0-7660-1782-6

El Niño & La Niña
Deadly Weather
ISBN 0-7660-1551-3

The Exxon Valdez
Tragic Oil Spill
ISBN 0-7660-1058-9

The Hindenburg Disaster
Doomed Airship
ISBN 0-7660-1554-8

Fire in Oakland, California
Billion-Dollar Blaze
ISBN 0-7660-1220-4

Hurricane Andrew
Nature's Rage
ISBN 0-7660-1057-0

Jonestown Massacre
Tragic End of a Cult
ISBN 0-7660-1789-2

Love Canal
Toxic Waste Tragedy
ISBN 0-7660-1553-X

Mount St. Helens Volcano
Violent Eruption
ISBN 0-7660-1552-1

The Oklahoma City Bombing
Terror in the Heartland
ISBN 0-7660-1061-9

Pearl Harbor
Deadly Surprise Attack
ISBN 0-7660-1783-4

Polio Epidemic
Crippling Virus Outbreak
ISBN 0-7660-1555-6

The Siege at Waco
Deadly Inferno
ISBN 0-7660-1218-2

The Titanic
Disaster at Sea
ISBN 0-7660-1557-2

Three Mile Island
Nuclear Disaster
ISBN 0-7660-1556-4

Triangle Shirtwaist Factory Fire
Flames of Labor Reform
ISBN 0-7660-1785-0

Tsunami
Monster Waves
ISBN 0-7660-1786-9

The World Trade Center Bombing
Terror in the Towers
ISBN 0-7660-1056-2

Jonestown Massacre

Tragic End of a Cult

Gina De Angelis

COLUMBIA CENTRAL H.S. LIBRARY
BROOKLYN, MICH.

AMERICAN
DISASTERS

Enslow Publishers, Inc.

40 Industrial Road   PO Box 38
Box 398   Aldershot
Berkeley Heights, NJ 07922   Hants GU12 6BP
USA   UK
http://www.enslow.com

The author wishes to sincerely thank Eva Weisbrod, friend and contributor, for her invaluable assistance with this book.

Copyright © 2002 by Enslow Publishers, Inc.

All rights reserved.

No part of this book may be reproduced by any means without the written permission of the publisher.

Library of Congress Cataloging-in-Publication Data

De Angelis, Gina.
    Jonestown massacre : tragic end of a cult / Gina De Angelis.
       p. cm. — (American disasters)
    Includes bibliographical references and index.
    Summary: Describes the life of Jim Jones and the church he established,
    supposedly to help people find a better life, and recounts the events
    that led to the deaths of Jones and his followers at their compound in
    Guyana in 1978.
    ISBN 0-7660-1784-2
    1. Jonestown Mass Suicide, Jonestown, Guyana, 1978—Juvenile
literature. [1. Jones, Jim, 1931-1978. 2. Cults. 3. Jonestown Mass
Suicide, Jonestown, Guyana, 1978.] I. Title. II. Series.
    BP605.P46 D43 2002
    988.1—dc21
                         2001007284

Printed in the United States of America

10 9 8 7 6 5 4 3 2 1

To Our Readers:
We have done our best to make sure all Internet Addresses in this book were active and appropriate when we went to press. However, the author and the publisher have no control over and assume no liability for the material available on those Internet sites or on other Web sites they may link to. Any comments or suggestions can be sent by e-mail to comments@enslow.com or to the address on the back cover.

Illustration Credits: AP/Wide World Photos, pp. 9, 10, 22, 33, 36; Bettmann/CORBIS, pp. 6, 15, 17; Chris Hardy/San Francisco Examiner, p. 41; Dino Vournas/Oakland Tribune, pp. 20, 40; Enslow Publishers, Inc., p. 24; Greg Robinson/San Francisco Examiner, pp. 26, 28; Lacy Atkins/San Francisco Examiner, pp. 1, 39; Roger Ressmeyer/CORBIS, p. 13; San Francisco Examiner, p. 35.

Cover Illustration: Bettmann/CORBIS.

Contents

*B*odies of cult members cover the floor of the main pavilion at Jonestown on November 20, 1978.

CHAPTER 1

Horror in the Jungle

There was no war in the country of Guyana, South America, on November 18, 1978. There was no deadly plague. Yet there, at the Jonestown Agricultural Settlement, lay hundreds of bodies. The Reverend Jim Jones and his followers, members of the Peoples Temple cult, were all dead.

Earlier that evening, Jones had called everyone together for a meeting. He told his congregation that it was time for everyone to die. "I haven't seen anybody yet didn't die. And I'd like to choose my own kind of death for a change," Jones said to the applause of his followers. Jones tape-recorded his last speech.[1]

One woman protested, but others shouted her down.[2] The group believed Jones. "To me death is not a fearful thing. It's living that's cursed," Jones said. Again, his followers applauded.[3]

Outside the main, open-sided building, staff members set up large kettles filled with grape Flavor-Aid, a drink made from a powdered mix. In the drink was a combination of potassium cyanide and a drug called Valium.[4] Cyanide is a chemical that is deadly in very small amounts. It causes death quickly but not instantly. Valium is a sedative. Sedatives relax you and make you sleepy. Jones planned that everyone would die quickly and painlessly.

Jones knew exactly what to do. He had babies and very small children killed first. Syringes, which doctors use to give shots, were filled with the juice. The syringes were emptied into the children's mouths. Older children were given cups of the liquid. Teenagers were served next, and then adults. Jones spoke into a microphone, telling parents to poison their children.

But death was neither quick nor painless. People had seizures. They foamed at the mouth and cried. A nurse called out to worried parents: "They're not crying from pain. It's just a little bitter tasting."[5] Jones, too, tried to reassure people, but the process was awful. The Valium did not work as fast as the cyanide. The first people were dead or dying before the rest got their drinks.

Odell Rhodes watched in horror. Rhodes was a follower of Jones, but he did not want to die. He walked out, pretending that he was running an errand for Jones. No one questioned him, because no one questioned authority at Jonestown. Jones encouraged his followers to think of him as a father figure. They had been taught to obey their "Dad" in all things. Away from the main area, Rhodes ran and hid under a building.

Another man, Stanley Clayton, also did not want to be part of Jones's plan. He escaped into the jungle surrounding Jonestown. He came back hours later, hoping the ordeal was over, to find his U.S. passport. He knew he would need it to leave Guyana.

Rhodes and Clayton were the only two people to run away that day, but there were other survivors. Grover Davis and Hyacinth Thrush survived in one of the houses. They had some-how slept through the whole thing.

Nine hundred and twelve people died from drinking poison. Two hundred seventy-six of the victims were young children.[6] Jones and one of his aides had both died of single gunshot wounds to the head. No one knows who shot whom.

By the time government officials from Guyana and the United States arrived at the remote village the next day, the bodies were already bloated and rotting in the jungle heat.

Crafts teacher Odell Rhodes witnessed the first twenty minutes of the massacre at Jonestown before managing to escape with his life.

More than twenty years later historians still argue about Jonestown. The most bitter arguments are about Jim Jones himself. He remains a mystery to many people.

Jim Jones spent most of his life leading the church he founded, Peoples Temple, first in Indiana and then in California. In the early 1970s, reporters began to hear dis-turbing things about Peoples Temple. Jones began telling his followers that the government was going to attack him. He had to move his church and its members for their own safety, he said. He found a safe place, he told them, in

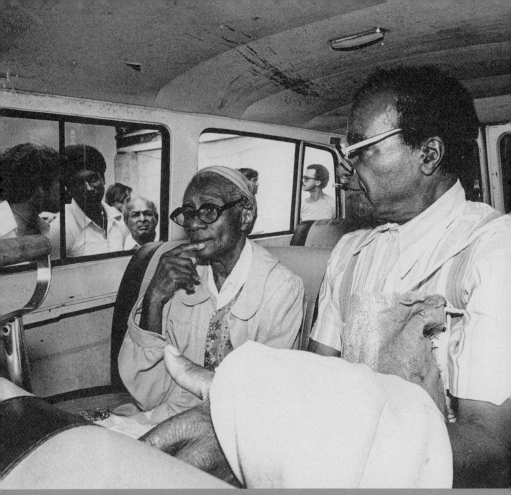

*H*yacinth Thrush, 84, and Grover Davis, 79, sit in the back of a van at Georgetown's Park Hotel, where they wait to be driven to the airport on November 29, 1978.

Guyana—a small country on the northeast coast of South America. Hundreds of people moved there with Jones beginning in 1977.

For a while, Jones and his followers felt their settlement, called Jonestown, was the Promised Land. But by 1978, Jonestown was failing. Still, the mass suicide that took place there stunned the outside world. How could it have happened?

CHAPTER 2

Who Was Jim Jones?

James Warren Jones was born May 13, 1931, in Crete, Indiana.[1] His father was disabled after fighting in World War I and could not work. Jim's mother, Lynetta, supported the family. They were poor, but Lynetta Jones taught her son to care about others. However, neighbors regarded her as an odd person. For example, she was suspicious of churches and what she called the "sky god."[2] Jim, too, was thought to be strange. He did not have many friends. But Jim was known for being kind, especially to stray animals.

In his teens, Jones got a job working in a hospital. There he met Marceline Baldwin, a nurse. Jones began attending Indiana University in January 1947, when he was only sixteen, but he already wanted to marry Marceline.[3] The two eventually wed in June 1949.

Marceline was from a strict Christian background, and was sometimes surprised by things Jones said. For example, he said he did not believe in God. He saw real suffering in the hospital, and he felt God was not helping the people there. Marceline disagreed. She wanted Jim to change his mind.

Marceline showed him a booklet about her church. Marceline's church was working for civil rights. It was an eye-opener for Jim. He had never seen a religious group that took action on matters he cared about. It changed his mind about God. He decided to become a minister.

In 1954, Jones became a student pastor at an Indianapolis church, the Laurel Street Tabernacle.[4] Soon he realized that this church was not helping the people he most wanted to help: African Americans. In the 1950s, churches were segregated. Jones did not approve of segregation, which kept African Americans separate from whites. He said, "I will not be a pastor of a black church or a white church. Wherever I have a church, *all* people will be welcome."[5]

Jim Jones preached emotionally to African Americans. He performed "healing" rituals: He told healthy people they had a serious illness, and then pretended to cure them. Eventually, Jones gained a following in Indianapolis. By 1956 he had enough followers to form his own church. He named it Peoples Temple. His church ran soup kitchens and organized home care for the sick and mentally ill.

In 1960, Peoples Temple joined the Disciples of Christ, a Christian group with a long and respected history. The members of Disciples of Christ believed in Jones's church and its programs. Peoples Temple then was called Peoples Temple Christian Church.

Barton Hunter, who was a friend of Jones and an official with Disciples of Christ, remembered Jones as an energetic man. He was always working on projects to help people. In 1964, Disciples of Christ ordained Jones as one of its ministers.[6] Before that, Jones was not officially a minister, even though he had many followers.

J im Jones in a photo taken on November 18, 1978.

Some of Jones's projects were related to communism. Jones was inspired by the writings of Karl Marx, the political philosopher behind communism. Jones believed that Marx's views were supported by the Bible—that everyone should contribute to the community what they could, and the community should take care of everyone according to their needs. In communism, which is a type of socialism, no one owns property. Instead, all of it belongs to the state or community. Individual people are not as important as the whole group.

Communism was under attack in America in the 1950s. Views like Jones's were extremely unpopular. Hunter knew this, but he felt that some of what Jones said was right. Hunter himself thought that people should be allowed to believe what they wanted, even if their views were unpopular.

Because of the support of respected people like Hunter and organizations like the Disciples of Christ, Jones was also respected. In these early days, Jones was so highly regarded in Indianapolis that the mayor gave him a significant job. The mayor made Jones Director of the city's Human Rights Commission. This job made Jones look even more important.

Jones worried about many things, especially the threat of nuclear war. He went on trips to find places he thought would be safe to live in case there was ever a nuclear war. There was also another reason Jones wanted to move. His "healings" had begun to attract unwanted attention. In late 1971, the State Board of Psychology Examiners in Indiana began investigating Jones. They decided that Jones's church was unusual, but that Jones's activities were not illegal. Faith healers, which is what Jones claimed to be, are protected under the First Amendment of the U.S. Constitution, which guarantees freedom of religion.

Protected or not, Jones did not want authorities watching him. He wanted to avoid all negative publicity, for fear of losing his followers and his career as a minister.

A town called Eureka looked promising. Eureka is on the northern coast of California. Jones told his followers that anyone living near Eureka would be safe from nuclear war no matter what happened to the rest of the country. He moved Peoples Temple to Ukiah, a town outside Eureka, in

Jim Jones and wife Marceline are pictured here preaching in California sometime in the early 1970s. The photo was taken from a photo album found in Jonestown shortly after the massacre.

1966. Sixty-five families (about 140 people) followed him there from Indianapolis.[7]

Ukiah was close enough to San Francisco that Jones could attract new members there. He started in African-American neighborhoods, but he did not ignore anyone. In 1966, Peoples Temple claimed a membership of eighty-six adults. In 1970, Peoples Temple opened another church in San Francisco. By then, Jones's church claimed to have 3,000 members.[8]

Most of the people who joined Peoples Temple in the early days were African Americans who were very poor and often troubled. Newer members in the 1970s were mostly people who were more successful. Many were educated and had good jobs. They joined the church because they felt Peoples Temple offered them a richer spiritual life.

Just like in Indiana, Jones was initially praised by local officials in California for his good works. Reporters wrote positive articles about him. Local citizens praised the good works of the members of Peoples Temple. They helped addicts give up drugs and find jobs. They started halfway houses to help the mentally ill and disabled. The church ran homes for foster children, the elderly, and the mentally retarded. State inspectors reported that the people who lived in these homes were all clean, well-fed, and happy.

During the late 1960s and early 1970s, Jones began to shift the focus of his church. He sensed that many of his new members did not appreciate his old-style preaching and claims to heal the sick. So he began to pay more attention to politics than religion.

Jones claimed the system in America was not taking care of all its citizens. Too many people, Jones said, had to struggle to make a little money, while others had far more money

Jim Jones leans on a stick while he observes an area being cleared for his Jonestown settlement.

than they needed. But members of Peoples Temple, Jones promised, would rise above that struggle.

For many who heard Jones preach, he answered every question they were asking themselves. He was concerned about the right problems and he seemed to know how to solve them.

CHAPTER 3

Building the Promised Land

When people joined Jones's church, they gave up their old way of life. New members of Peoples Temple gave a big part of their income to the church, and they often lived in one of the church-owned houses. Eventually members would give all of their income to Peoples Temple. The church needed the money, Jones explained, to maintain its programs. Jones also bought a fleet of buses so he and his followers could travel around the country, spreading his word and finding new members. It was hard work for church members. But Jones told people that anything good in life required sacrifices. The people who joined Jones agreed with him wholeheartedly. They devoted their lives and all their property to Jones's church.

About seven out of every ten church members were African American. This high proportion of minorities has led some reporters and historians to assume that most Peoples Temple members were poor. But many of the church's African-American members were far from poor. Some had been active in the fight for civil rights. They believed, as Jones did, in communal living. This is why they joined the church—not because they needed money or a new religion.

Peoples Temple attracted people from all walks of life. African Americans, whites, the young, the old, and the middle-aged all became members. The one thing all members had in common was a belief that by joining Jones they would be working together toward a greater good, and building a better world. Jones called this "the Cause."[1]

Members of Peoples Temple were, like Jones, devoted to racial equality. Jones practiced what he preached. While still in Indiana, he and Marceline adopted an African-American child—the first time in Indiana history that a white couple adopted a child of color. The Joneses adopted more children from other ethnic backgrounds. As their family grew, so did Peoples Temple. The Joneses called themselves a rainbow family.[2]

Another way Jones proved his commitment to racial equality was in the communal houses for Peoples Temple members. At a time when segregation was all many Americans had ever known, African Americans and whites lived there together happily. This arrangement and Jones's own multiracial family were two of the most exceptional things about Peoples Temple.

Often, entire families would join the church. One person would hear Jones giving a speech, be drawn in, and encourage his or her relatives to join. One example of this was Tim Stoen, a successful young lawyer. He worked in the district attorney's office in Mendocino County, in northern California. He was hoping to become director of the Legal Services Foundation there in 1967, when he met Jones, who was on the board of directors.

J im Jones, Jr., is comforted by his wife, Erin, during a memorial service for the Jonestown victims that took place in Oakland, California, in 1998. The Joneses were the first white couple in Indiana history to adopt an African-American child.

Stoen joined Peoples Temple in 1969. He immediately began to work for the church as a lawyer. His girlfriend, Grace, was uncomfortable with Jones and Peoples Temple, but Tim convinced her of their value. In 1970, Grace and Tim married in the church, and Grace became a member. She soon joined the church staff. The Stoens helped the church expand further, to Los Angeles. Tim Stoen believed in Jones's work so much that when Grace gave birth to their son, John Victor Stoen, Tim signed a document stating that the true father of the child was Jones. He said Jones should have custody—the legal right to care for the child. This meant that the Stoens gave up the right to raise John Victor.

It is hard to believe that any parent would give up their child like this. But the Stoens did. They did it because they believed in Jim Jones. Their unquestioning devotion to their religious leader is the definition of cult behavior. This kind of behavior is the result of the effect a powerful personality, like that of Jim Jones. Such a personality can sometimes convince other people to do almost anything.[3] Followers might believe that their leader is personally in touch with God, and that loyalty to God is shown by loyalty to the leader, himself.

This type of extreme devotion can lead people to make bad decisions. Members of a religious group whose leader requires absolute devotion will follow bad advice from that leader to show their loyalty. They may even believe the advice is good, because the leader says it is good. The Stoens' giving up their son is a good example of this.

Psychologists and others have long debated why people join cults. Some believe that those who join cults are weak personalities who crave the strong guidance that some religious groups seem to offer. Others believe that there is no single type of personality that is drawn to cults. The history of Peoples Temple seems to support this view. Jones's followers included a wide variety of people. All they had in common was a search for happiness and fulfillment.

During the early 1970s, the Peoples Temple organization became more complex. As more people joined and gave their life savings and property to Peoples Temple, the church dealt with more money than ever. The church appeared to be thriving. Jones grew paranoid, however. This means he thought that people were "after" him.

Some reporters in the San Francisco Bay Area had heard that there were problems at Peoples Temple. People who had left the church were called defectors. They told stories about children being beaten, and about sexual abuse in the church. Some told reporters that Jones was crazy.

*T*im Stoen admires an old photo of his son, John Stoen, in 1988. John lost his life in the Jonestown massacre that took place ten years earlier.

Some defectors described sessions called "Catharsis." During these church sessions, people were accused of wrong-doing. The whole congregation would vote on their guilt or innocence. If they were voted guilty, they could be beaten, forced to fight large, strong church members, or punished in other hurtful, embarrassing ways. Jones was said to direct all of these sessions.[4]

Many defectors also said that Jones had made members sign papers saying they were guilty of crimes or other bad things. Jones had told them that they must sign to prove their loyalty to him and the group. The Stoens later claimed that the paper they signed giving Jones custody of their son was one example of this. Sometimes church members signed blank pages. Then Jones could write anything he wanted on the pages, and the signatures would make it look as if the members agreed with what the papers said.[5]

Jones claimed that the stories were all lies. Reporters tried to interview him, but Jones would not talk to them. He used his influence with local officials—and sometimes threats—to prevent negative articles from being printed. Defectors claimed they were sometimes threatened, too. But these claims were difficult to prove. Jones remained well-respected.

As the church grew less religious and more political, Jones began telling his followers that the Bible was full of lies. He began using the word "sky god" to describe the God that Christians and others believed in. Soon, he began to claim that he, Jones, was the only true god.

Jones suffered from extreme paranoia, which may have been caused partly by his drug abuse or could have resulted from mental illness. Jones took many drugs that kept him awake for hours and hours. Then he could watch over everyone and ensure their proper behavior. But the drugs almost certainly unbalanced his mind. His rage and mood swings began to frighten people.[6]

Marceline, who was a nurse and helped administer Jones's drugs, understood their effects. She worried about her husband, but she also feared him. Jones watched Marceline's behavior perhaps even more closely than other Temple members. Jones also formed close relationships with other women, and Marceline became jealous.

Marceline's hurt feelings grew deeper over time, but she stood by her husband to the very end.

In the early 1970s, Jones began to talk about how the government was after him. He said the Federal Bureau of Investigation (FBI) and the Central Intelligence Agency (CIA) were watching Peoples Temple. According to some members who later left the church, Jones was growing more and more nervous and paranoid.

Jones told his followers he planned to move Peoples Temple to another country, where they would all be safe. After years of searching, he found the right place: the South American country of Guyana.

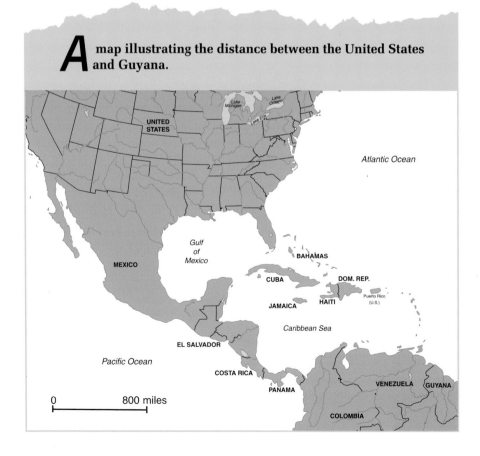

A map illustrating the distance between the United States and Guyana.

CHAPTER 4

Jonestown

In 1973, Jim Jones began to arrange for the Jonestown Agricultural Settlement in Georgetown, Guyana. It was far enough from the United States to make Jones feel safe, but still close enough to quickly fly back to the U.S., if necessary. The Guyanese government was happy to lease 3,000 acres of jungle land to Peoples Temple.[1]

Construction began immediately. Since Guyana was not a wealthy country like the United States, everything had to be imported and shipped to Jonestown—including food, clothes, and lumber for buildings. By the end of 1975, the settlement was just beginning to take shape. Even in early 1977, only fifty people lived there. Still, the settlement was working and the people were happy.[2]

Later in 1977, Jones learned he was being investigated in the U.S. for not paying taxes. Now he wanted to move to Guyana immediately. He urged his followers to move too. When the first Temple members began arriving at Jonestown, they were happy and excited. By early 1978, nearly a thousand people were living there.

Doris Lewis was among the many Temple members to relocate to Jonestown in 1978. She and her husband, Fred

Lewis, were both Baptists until Doris first heard of the Temple through friends and joined. She tried to get her husband to join the Temple with her, but he refused. "I never did believe in this man [Jones]," Fred Lewis would later recall. "Any time a man starts talking about [how] he is God, and [that] you should throw away the Bible . . . I don't want anything to do with him."[3]

One Saturday night in August 1978, Fred Lewis came home from his job as a butcher and found his family's San Francisco apartment cleaned out. His wife and seven children were gone. Lewis later learned that his wife, with

*T*he main road leading into the Jonestown settlement in Guyana. The sign reads "Welcome to Jonestown: Peoples Temple Agricultural Project."

the help of other Temple members, had packed up nearly all of their furniture and moved with the children to Guyana.

"She left me one mattress and no note," Lewis remembered. "I thought they'd been kidnapped. . . . I went [back] to work and told them my family was gone and they all said, 'Fred, you're kidding.' I was crying, but everybody told me it's not true, they'll be back."[4]

As more people relocated to Guyana, problems arose. It was hard to get supplies to the settlement. Not enough buildings had been built. Many people were not used to the jungle heat and some grew sick. The church was wealthy, but Jones would not always spend the money for necessary items. The houses, which were really big cabins with rows of bunk beds, were overcrowded.[5] Jonestown soon began to deteriorate.

Some members began to feel that Jonestown was not the "Promised Land" they thought it would be. In addition to the overcrowded cabins and poor food, married couples had to sleep in separate places. Everyone had to work up to eleven hours a day, six days a week. On Sundays they worked eight hours. Nights were for church meetings, at which Jones spoke endlessly. Sometimes after everyone was finally allowed to sleep, Jones still would ramble on and on over the loudspeakers, keeping people awake.

"You've seen me raise the dead," Jones would say, "seen those who were blind open their eyes, seen the crippled suddenly made whole, seen them pass cancer after cancer. . . . I'm incarnate. I'm a liberator. I'm a savior. I am that which they call God."[6]

Few visitors were allowed into Jonestown, but the American ambassador to Guyana was one. Before any visitors came, Jones told members how to act to make a

*J*onestown residents applaud after a performance by the camp rock group, the Jonestown Express, on November 17, 1978. Jim Jones stands at the far end of the table.

good impression. During visits, people got better food, including meat.

Even today, some people claim that most of the members at Jonestown were very happy. They felt their "cause" was a good one. But it is certain that others were very unhappy. Some of them tried to escape from Jonestown, but few succeeded. Armed guards around the settlement supposedly protected the church from outside "enemies." But these guards also kept members from leaving.

Back in the U.S., a group called Concerned Relatives wrote to government officials asking for help to bring their relatives home from Jonestown. Defectors kept telling stories of abuse, making the relatives even more worried.

The most famous defectors were the Stoens. Tim and Grace Stoen had left Peoples Temple and wanted their son, John, returned to them.[7] They sued Jim Jones for custody. In September 1977, the California court issued a warrant for the arrest of John Stoen. Even though the boy had done nothing wrong, authorities knew that by arresting him he would be declared a ward of the court. That meant the state would take care of him until the legal fight was over. Unfortunately, as long as Jim Jones held John Stoen in Guyana, he remained beyond the reach of U.S. authorities. John Stoen would become one of the many innocent children to lose their lives in Jonestown.

Because Jones had ignored earlier court statements to return John Stoen, Jones was declared in contempt of court. That meant he could be arrested if he ever went back to the U.S. This made Jones even more nervous that the government really was trying to destroy him.

It was at this point that Jones began training his followers to commit suicide. Over the loudspeakers, Jones demanded that everyone meet immediately, often in the middle of the night. Jones called these "White Nights." He told his followers they were under attack, and they must all drink poisoned juice. The juice was not really poisoned, but the people did not know that until the expected death never came. It was a test of their loyalty, Jones said afterwards.[8]

In May 1978, Debbie Layton Blakey escaped from Jonestown. She told government officials about the suicide drills. She was afraid for her life even after she escaped. She was also worried about her brother and mother, who were still in Jonestown.[9]

A man named Leon Broussard also managed to escape. He said church members were starved or put in an underground hole when Jones got angry with them. If he was extremely angry with someone, Broussard said, Jones would have the person drugged to keep him from causing more "trouble."[10]

Just as they did in California, church members in Jonestown beat each other if Jones commanded it. Ten-year-old Tracy Parks later recalled that "children who said they were not happy and wanted to go away were severely beaten." One twelve-year-old girl was "kept imprisoned for weeks in a plywood box three feet wide, four feet high and six feet long."[11]

Congressman Leo Ryan from San Mateo, California, was one of several politicians who had been alarmed by the stories he had heard about Jonestown. In late 1978, he decided to go to Guyana and judge the conditions there in person.

Ambush

On Tuesday, November 14, 1978, Congressman Ryan, seventeen of the Concerned Relatives, a few newspaper reporters, and an NBC-TV team flew to Georgetown, Guyana. It took several days to get permission to enter Jonestown. Jones tried to keep out the Concerned Relatives, but they refused to leave Guyana without seeing their family members. Jones then said he was ill and could not have guests. He made up excuses to stall for time. Finally he let Ryan and the others into Jonestown on Friday, November 17.

At first, things looked fine. San Francisco reporter Charles Krause described Jonestown as "spotless" and "impressive."[1] The main pavilion had a tin roof and open sides. On the stage was an armchair with a microphone, where Jones would sit. Above it was a large sign that read, "Those who do not remember the past are condemned to repeat it." That evening the camp rock group, the Jonestown Express, performed for Ryan and the others. Children played together happily. Everyone sat down together for dinner. The food was good.

But as they looked around further, the visitors began to notice odd behavior. Everyone called Jones "Father" or

"Dad." They all seemed to be acting unnaturally.[2] People did not appear to think for themselves. Congressman Ryan and the other visitors became concerned.

Jones agreed to speak with Ryan and the reporters after dinner. Jones looked sick, and took a lot of pills while he talked. He wore heavy makeup and looked as if he dyed his hair. Jones denied all the stories of abuse. He claimed the U.S. government was attacking him because they wanted the "cause" to fail. He said there were plots against him and his church. It had also been discovered that weapons were stockpiled at Jonestown. Jones claimed that these weapons were only there to defend the settlement.

The following morning, Jones was still insisting that everyone was free to leave whenever they wanted. Ryan told Jones that if anyone wanted to leave, they could fly back to the United States with him. Jones again denied that anyone wanted to leave. Then NBC-TV correspondent Don Harris handed Jones a note that had been slipped to him the night before. Two people at Jonestown had written "help us get out of Jonestown," along with their names, on a piece of paper.

Jones was very angry. He glared at Harris when the reporter showed him the note. "People play games, friend," Jones told Harris. "They lie. Are you people going to leave us? I just beg you, please leave us."[3]

Jackie Speier was a legal aide to Congressman Ryan who had accompanied him on his visit to Jonestown. After seeing the note, she knew that "there was fear and intimidation, that the reception was a charade, [and] that people were being held against their will."[4]

Ryan and Speier began to question the Jonestown residents, asking if any of them would like to leave. Eventually, one elderly woman stepped forward and said she wanted to leave with Ryan. Her courage inspired the rest of her family. Several more residents soon stepped forward as well.

"My most vivid memory—it's one that haunts me still—is of a couple pulling on the arms of their child, who was three or four," Speier later recalled. "One parent wanted to leave; the other wanted to stay, and the child was caught [in] between."[5]

In all, there were sixteen people who said they wanted to leave with Ryan. Among them was Larry Layton, the brother of defector Debbie Layton Blakey. Before leaving, he was seen hugging Jones. Strangely, he did not bother to hug or kiss his wife, Karen, who was staying behind. Layton also took no baggage with him as he accompanied the other defectors into the truck that was to take them to the airport at Port Kaituma.

Congressman Ryan said he would stay behind and wait a while longer in case anyone else wanted to go. The truck

*H*eroic Congressman Leo J. Ryan tried to help others escape Jonestown in November 1978.

had just left when shouts were heard from the settlement. Ryan suddenly appeared with blood on his shirt. Inside the settlement, a man had tried to slit his throat, but Ryan wrenched free. He was unhurt—the blood was from his attacker, who had cut himself in the struggle.

Ryan joined the now fearful group as they hurried to the waiting airplanes at Port Kaituma. Once there, Speier expressed concern to Ryan about Larry Layton. She knew that Layton had previously denounced his sister for defecting. "I was fearful about being on the same aircraft as Larry Layton. I told Leo Ryan I thought he was a fraud."[6]

The Twin Otter that was scheduled to take the Ryan party had only nineteen seats, so a second plane, a Cessna, was chartered for the defectors. At first, Layton managed to avoid the body search other passengers were subjected to. Once aboard the Cessna, one of the newspaper reporters pointed out that Layton had not been searched. Layton climbed back out of the plane and was frisked. No weapons were found on him.

The Cessna was about to take off when suddenly a tractor-trailer drove out of the jungle. Aboard the trailer were members of Peoples Temple, who began shooting. NBC cameraman Bob Brown was killed by a short-range shotgun blast. He may have survived had he tried to escape, but he kept filming until he was shot. Congressman Ryan, Don Harris, defector Patricia Parks, and photographer Greg Robinson were also shot to death in front of the Twin Otter plane. Eleven others, including Jackie Speier, were wounded.[7]

"I was lying on the ground by one of the plane's wheels, pretending to be dead," Speier later remembered. "I had my head on my arm, but I was one of the people they targeted, and was shot five times in the shoulder and right side by guys with rifles and shotguns. . . . I went into shock. My

San Francisco *Examiner* photographer Greg Robinson rides into the Jonestown settlement along with Bob Flick of NBC-TV (left) in November 1978.

mind rejected what had happened. Once I comprehended it I thought, 'I never expected to die at such an early age—I was twenty-eight at the time. Would my parents ever know?'"[8]

At first, the Cessna pilot aborted takeoff when he saw the assault on the Twin Otter. Suddenly, Larry Layton drew a gun and began firing. He had probably hidden the weapon beneath his seat when he first boarded the plane. He wounded two defectors before the gun was wrestled away from him.

Now the Cessna took off, with a subdued Layton and the two wounded defectors among others on board. Some of the other defectors who were left behind scattered into the jungle. Reporter Charles Krause gave Speier his shirt to help stop her bleeding.

"We all thought we were goners," said Speier. "We thought the hit squad would come back and finish us off."[9]

Speier found shelter in a tent with several other survivors of the assault. Some of the defectors left among them said the "White Night" ritual that they had rehearsed so many times was probably now under way. They were right.

"We must die with dignity. Hurry, hurry, hurry," Jones told church members back at the settlement. "We must hurry. . . . Death is a million times preferable to ten more days of this life."[10]

Armed soldiers stand guard at the airstrip in Port Kaituma, Guyana on Monday, November 20, 1978. In the background is the bullet-ridden Twin Otter plane that was to carry Congressman Ryan two days earlier.

CHAPTER 6

"Jones Took My Family"

Jackie Speier was lucky to survive that terrifying night in the jungle. "I was shot five times and still have two bullets in my body," she later said. "I could easily have been shot dead." It was sometime after midnight when Speier learned that everyone in Jonestown was dead. A plane from Georgetown, Guyana, finally arrived to rescue Speier and the other survivors on Sunday afternoon. By Monday, Speier was in surgery.[1]

Fred Lewis was at work when he heard the shocking news of the massacre. "[A] man came running in and said Congressman Leo Ryan was killed," Lewis remembered. "I dropped my tools, ran home, and there on the TV they were showing those awful pictures of the people lying on the ground, and rolling those names of the dead. My family was on it."[2]

In addition to his wife and seven children, Lewis also lost nineteen other relatives at Jonestown—more relatives than anyone else had lost. They are buried, along with 379 other victims, at Evergreen Cemetery in Oakland, California. There is a separate stone marker for Lewis's twenty-seven family members. "That man Jones took my family," Lewis said in 1998, still suffering his tremendous loss twenty years later. "It is always with me, always."[3]

After the massacre at Jonestown, members of Peoples Temple still in the United States defended Jim Jones, claiming that Peoples Temple was not a cult. The Peoples Temple, nevertheless, fell apart. As time passed, most survivors became active in more mainstream churches. In the years after 1978, the American public became more suspicious of unusual religious groups. The word "cult" took on an even more negative meaning in most people's minds.

After several years as a county supervisor, Jackie Speier ran for the Assembly seat once held by Leo Ryan and won. By incredible coincidence, she was sworn in on the same day in 1986 that Larry Layton was convicted of aiding and abetting in Ryan's assassination. Layton is now serving a life term in prison. In 1998, Speier was elected as a California state senator.

In the 1990s, other horrific events inspired by religious or spiritual feeling have reignited suspicions of cults. These events are always compared to Jonestown, which remains the largest cult-related disaster in American history. It is the yardstick by which all other cult events are measured.

In November 1998, a twentieth anniversary memorial service was held in Oakland, California, to honor the memory of the Jonestown victims. Fred Lewis and Jackie Speier were among those in attendance, along with two of Jones's surviving adult children, Jim, Jr., and Stephan Jones—both men had been in Georgetown, away from the settlement, when the massacre took place. At the service, Speier reflected on the legacy of Jonestown.

"Cults are here to stay. The menace still lingers," she

S tate Senator-elect Jackie Speier stands alongside Fred Lewis during the twentieth anniversary memorial service for the Jonestown victims that took place at Oakland's Evergreen Cemetery in November 1998.

said. "It's arrogant to believe something like this couldn't happen again."[4]

Some scholars, such as J. Gordon Melton, founder of the Institute for the Study of American Religion in Santa Barbara, California, warn against misjudging new religious movements out of fear of cults. "[Jonestown is] the story of a mainline church gone bad, not a new religion," Melton said. "[Many people] believe that all these groups are bad and brainwash their members." In Melton's view, "brainwashing doesn't exist."[5]

Other scholars, such as Margaret Singer, a professor of

psychology at the University of California at Berkeley, disagree. They believe dangerous cults are easy to distinguish from legitimate religions. "[Cult leaders] see how easy it is to pick up the lonely and the depressed and sell them a bill of goods," Singer said. "There are so many people out there looking for easy answers to life's complicated problems."[6]

Jackie Speier agreed with this view. "Many of the Peoples Temple members. . . . were searching for love. They were fragile people whose lives were incomplete.

*S*tephan Jones kneels beside a commemorative stone honoring the Jonestown victims during the memorial service held in Oakland in November 1998.

*T*ourists view photographs at the Jonestown exhibit in San Francisco's temporary City Hall in 1998.

Cults attract people who are searching for some meaning in their life.

"I bristle when people say Jonestown was a 'mass suicide,'" Speier added. "Hundreds of people, including the children, were murdered!"[7]

No one has ever been satisfied with explanations for the tragedy at Jonestown. Arguments continue even today, but the view held by most scholars is that the horror of Jonestown was not a suicide, but indeed a mass murder—a religious movement gone horribly wrong.

Other Cult-Related Disasters

DATE	PLACE	EVENT
April 19, 1993	Waco, Texas	Seventy-two members of a cult led by David Koresh, including Koresh himself, are killed when their compound near Waco, Texas, is set afire. Among the dead were twenty-two children. The fire is believed to have been started by cult members. It came at the end of a fifty-one-day standoff by the Bureau of Alcohol, Tobacco and Firearms (ATF) and the Federal Bureau of Investigation (FBI), who wanted to inspect Koresh's compound for illegally held weapons and alleged child abuse.
October 1994	Switzerland and Canada	Fifty-three Solar Temple members are found burned to death. The Solar Temple had numerous legal problems in several countries; it is thought that these woes hastened the suicides. Forty-eight members died in Switzerland, and five in Quebec, Canada.
1994–1995	Japan	Sarin gas is released by members of the Aum Shinrikyo cult in the streets of Matsumoto, Japan, in June 1994; seven people die. In March 1995, they release sarin gas in a Tokyo subway during rush hour. Twelve people die and thousands are injured. Aum Shinrikyo was founded in Japan in 1984 by Shoko Asahara. Asahara believed that 30,000 people must have their souls saved by joining his temple, or else the world would not have enough spiritually awakened people to avert disaster by nuclear war in 1999. In January 2000, Aum Shinrikyo changed its name to Aleph to try to improve its public image.
March 1997	San Diego, California	Thirty-nine members of the "Heaven's Gate" cult, led by Marshall Applewhite, kill themselves at their communal home in Rancho Santa Fe, near San Diego. The suicides followed the cult members' belief that they must shed their earthly bodies ("containers") to meet a spaceship in the comet Hale-Bopp. In May 1997, two more members of the cult attempted suicide; one succeeded and the other succeeded on another attempt in February 1998.
March 2000	Uganda, Africa	More than 235 members of Restoration of the Ten Commandments of God commit suicide. The group was found dead in their burned church in southwestern Uganda. Reporters noted that the church had been boarded up and that there was no sign of struggle. The suicide appeared to have been inspired by the belief of the leader, Joseph Kibweteere, that the world would end in December 1999. When that prediction failed to come true, he changed the date to December 2000.

Chapter Notes

Chapter 1. Horror in the Jungle

1. Mary McCormick Maaga, "'Death Tape' Transcription," *Alternative Consideration of Jonestown & People's Temple*, July 26, 2001, <http://www-rohan.sdsu.edu/~remoore/jonestown /tapes/Q042maaga.html> (October 26, 2001).

2. Min Yee and Thomas N. Layton, *In My Father's House: The Story of the Layton Family and the Reverend Jim Jones* (New York: Berkley Publishing Co., 1982), pp. 307–308.

3. Mary McCormick Maaga, "'Death Tape' Transcription."

4. Ethan Feinsod, *Awake in a Nightmare* (New York: Norton, 1981), p. 188.

5. Tim Reiterman and John Jacobs, *Raven: The Untold Story of the Rev. Jim Jones and His People* (New York: E.P. Dutton, 1982), p. 96.

6. Kathleen Kinsolving and Tom Kinsolving, "Madman in Our Midst: Jim Jones and the California Coverup," *Freedom of Mind*, 1998, <http://www.freedomofmind.com/groups/temple/ madman.htm> (May 24, 2001).

Chapter 2. Who Was Jim Jones?

1. John R. Hall, *Gone from the Promised Land: Jonestown in American Cultural History* (New Brunswick, N.J.: Transaction Books, 1987), p. 6.

2. Ibid., p. 10.

3. Tim Reiterman and John Jacobs, *Raven: The Untold Story of the Rev. Jim Jones and His People* (New York: E.P. Dutton, 1982), p. 34.

4. Hall, p. 42.

5. Ibid.

6. Ibid., p. 52.

7. Reiterman and Jacobs, p. 98.

8. Ibid., pp. 156, 267.

Chapter 3. Building the Promised Land

1. Mary McCormick Maaga, *Hearing the Voices of Jonestown* (Syracuse, N.Y.: Syracuse University Press, 1998), pp. 145–146.

2. Mary McCormick Maaga, "Three Gangs In One," *Alternative Consideration of Jonestown & People's Temple*, Spring 1998, <http://www-rohan.sdsu.edu/~remoore/jonestown /articles/three.html> (October 26, 2001).

3. "Cults 101," *Apologetics Index*, n.d., <http://www. gospelcom.net/apologeticsindex/c09.html#defcults> (October 26, 2001).

4. Marshall Kilduff and Ron Javers, *The Suicide Cult* (New York: Bantam Books, 1978), p. 64.

5 Jeannie Mills, *Six Years With God: Life Inside Reverend Jim Jones's Peoples Temple* (New York: A & W Publishers, 1979), pp. 11–12, 25–26, 95.

6 Kathleen Kinsolving and Tom Kinsolving, "Madman in Our Midst: Jim Jones and the California Coverup," *Freedom of Mind*, 1998, <http://www.freedomofmind.com/groups/temple/ madman.htm> (May 24, 2001).

Chapter 4. Jonestown

1. Tim Reiterman and John Jacobs, *Raven: The Untold Story of the Rev. Jim Jones and His People* (New York: E.P. Dutton, 1982), p. 239.

2. John R. Hall, *Gone from the Promised Land: Jonestown in American Cultural History* (New Brunswick, N.J.: Transaction Books, 1987), p. 73.

3. Kevin Fagan, "Haunted by Memories of Hell," *San Francisco Chronicle*, November 12, 1998, p. A1.

4. Ibid.

5. Marshall Kilduff and Ron Javers, *The Suicide Cult* (New York: Bantam Books, 1978), p. 158.

6. Maitland Zane, "Surviving the Heart of Darkness," *San Francisco Chronicle*, November 13, 1998, p. A1.

7. Reiterman and Jacobs, p. 292.

8. Ibid., pp. 293–296.

9. Deborah Layton, *Seductive Poison: A Jonestown Survivor's Story of Life and Death in the Peoples Temple* (New York: Doubleday, 1998), pp. 277–278.

10. Reiterman and Jacobs, p. 449.

11. Kathleen Kinsolving and Tom Kinsolving, "Madman in Our Midst: Jim Jones and the California Coverup," *Freedom of Mind*, 1998, <http://www.freedomofmind.com/groups/temple/madman.htm> (May 24, 2001).

Chapter 5. Ambush

1. Charles Krause, *The Guyana Massacre: The Eyewitness Account* (New York: Berkley Publishing Co., 1978), p. 66.

2. Ibid., p. 37.

3. Maitland Zane, "Surviving the Heart of Darkness," *San Francisco Chronicle*, November 13, 1998, p. A1.

4. Ibid.

5. Ibid.

6. Ibid.

7 Kathleen Kinsolving and Tom Kinsolving, "Madman in Our Midst: Jim Jones and the California Coverup," *Freedom of Mind*, 1998, <http://www.freedomofmind.com/groups/temple/madman.htm> (May 24, 2001).

8. Zane, p. A1.

9. Ibid.

10. Mary McCormick Maaga, *Hearing the Voices of Jonestown* (Syracuse, N.Y.: Syracuse University Press, 1998), p. 162.

Chapter 6. "Jones Took My Family"

1. Maitland Zane, "Surviving the Heart of Darkness," *San Francisco Chronicle*, November 13, 1998, p. A1.

2. Kevin Fagan, "Haunted by Memories of Hell," *San Francisco Chronicle*, November 12, 1998, p. A1.

3. Ibid.

4. Zane, p. A1.

5. Don Lattin, "The End To Innocent Acceptance Of Sects: Sharper Scrutiny is Jonestown Legacy," *San Francisco Chronicle*, November 13, 1998, p. A1.

6. Ibid.

7. Zane, p. A1.

civil rights—Rights an individual is entitled to as a citizen.

communal living—When a group of people live together as equals. Everyone's money and goods belong to the group, and work is shared by all members.

communism—A system in which no one owns his or her own property; instead, all property belongs to the state or community. In a communist system, the group is more important than the individual.

cult—A group devoted to extreme beliefs, or religious veneration of a particular person.

custody—The legal right to care for a child.

defector—Someone who was once loyal to, but then leaves, a group, person or cause.

ordain—To officially declare someone as a minister of a church.

paranoia—A mental illness characterized by believing that people are "out to get" the sufferer.

passport—A document stating that one is a citizen of a certain country. It is needed for travel between nations.

sedative—A drug that makes someone relaxed or sleepy.

segregation—The systematic separation of people, for example, by color or gender.

socialism—A political philosophy that believes that the government should control the distribution of property and the means of production.

Further Reading

Cole, Michael D. *The Siege at Waco.* Berkeley Heights, N.J.: Enslow Publishers, Inc., 1999.

Dolan, Sean. *Everything You Need to Know about Cults.* New York: Rosen Publishing Group, 2000.

Goodnough, David. *Cult Awareness: A Hot Issue.* Berkeley Heights, N.J.: Enslow Publishers, Inc., 2000.

Karson, Jill. *Cults.* San Diego, Calif.: Greenhaven Press, 2000.

Maaga, Mary McCormick. *Hearing the Voices of Jonestown.* Syracuse, N.Y.: Syracuse University Press, 1998.

Internet Addresses

Alternative Consideration of Jonestown & Peoples Temple
http://www-rohan.sdsu.edu/~remoore/jonestown/

Jonestown Massacre +20: Questions Linger
http://www1.cnn.com/US/9811/18/jonestown.anniv.01/

Jonestown: Examining the Peoples Temple
http://www.owlnet.rice.edu/~reli291/Jonestown/Jonestown.html

The Jonestown Massacre
http://www.crimelibrary.com/serial4/jonestown/index.html/